JESUS
and His Early Ministry

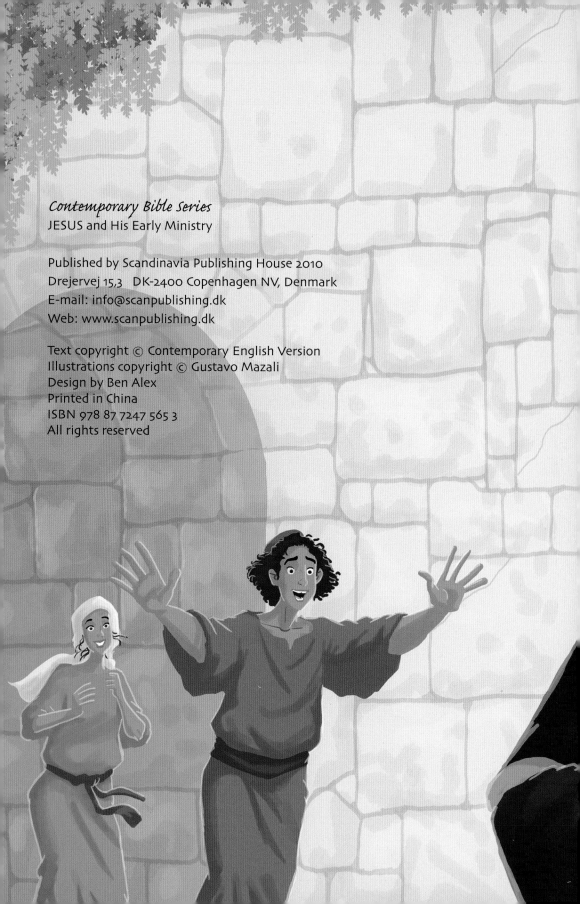

Contemporary Bible Series
JESUS and His Early Ministry

Published by Scandinavia Publishing House 2010
Drejervej 15,3   DK-2400 Copenhagen NV, Denmark
E-mail: info@scanpublishing.dk
Web: www.scanpublishing.dk

Text copyright © Contemporary English Version
Illustrations copyright © Gustavo Mazali
Design by Ben Alex
Printed in China
ISBN 978 87 7247 565 3

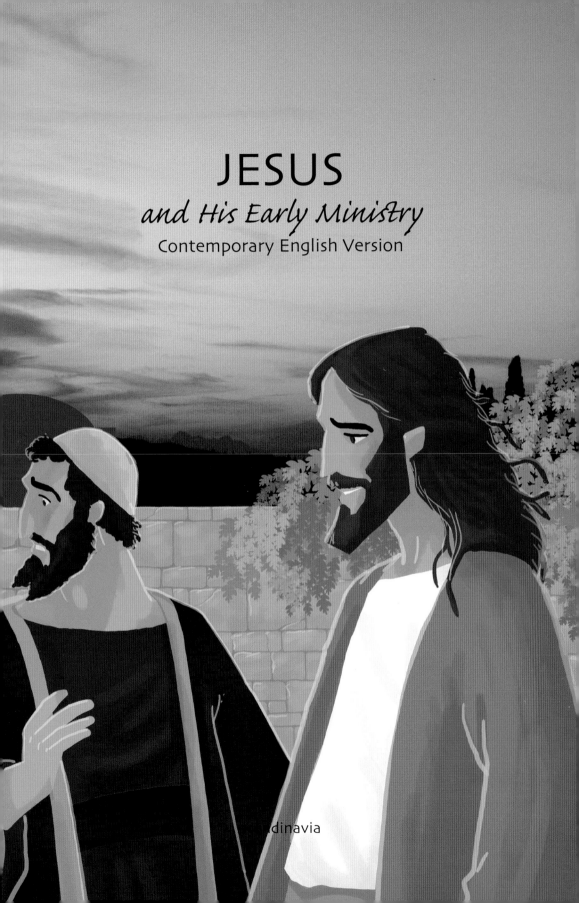

JESUS
and His Early Ministry
Contemporary English Version

dinavia

Contents

An Angel Visits Zechariah

Luke 1:5-25

When Herod was king of Judea, there was a priest by the name of Zechariah. His wife Elizabeth was from the family of Aaron. Both of them were good people and pleased the Lord. Zechariah and Elizabeth were old, but they did not have children.

One day Zechariah was serving God in the temple as a priest. All at once an angel from the Lord appeared to Zechariah at the right side of the altar. Zechariah was confused and afraid when he saw the angel.

The angel told him, "Don't be afraid, Zechariah! Your wife Elizabeth will have a son, and you must name him John. Your son will be a great servant of the Lord. John will lead many people in Israel to turn back to the Lord their God. Because of John, parents will be more thoughtful of their children. People who now disobey God will begin to think as they ought to. That is how John will get people ready for the Lord."

Zechariah said to the angel, "How will I know this is going to happen? My wife and I are both very old." The angel answered,

"I am Gabriel, God's servant, and I was sent to tell you this good news. You have not believed what I have said. But everything will take place when it is supposed to."

When Zechariah's time of service in the temple was over, he went home. Soon after that, his wife was expecting a baby. For five months she did not leave the house. She said to herself, "What the Lord has done for me will keep people from looking down on me."

4

An Angel Visits Mary

Luke 1:26-38

One month later God sent the angel Gabriel to the town of Nazareth in Galilee with a message for a virgin named Mary. She was engaged to Joseph from the family of King David. The angel greeted Mary and said, "You are truly blessed! The Lord is with you." Mary was confused by the angel's words. She wondered what they meant. Then the angel told Mary, "Don't be afraid! God is pleased with you, and you will have a son. His name will be Jesus. He will be great and will be called the Son of God Most High. The Lord God will make him king, as his ancestor David was. He will rule the people of Israel forever. His kingdom will never end."

Mary asked the angel, "How can this happen? I am not married!"

The angel answered, "The Holy Spirit will come down to you, and God's power will come over you. Your child will be called the holy Son of God. Your relative Elizabeth is also going to have a son, even though she is old. No one thought she could ever have a baby, but in three months she will have a son. Nothing is impossible for God!"

Mary said, "I am the Lord's servant! Let it happen as you have said."

Then the angel left her.

Mary Visits Elizabeth
Luke 1:39-45

A short time later Mary hurried to
a town in the hill country of Judea.
She went into Zechariah's home,
where she greeted Elizabeth.
When Elizabeth heard Mary's
greeting, her baby moved within
her. The Holy Spirit came upon
Elizabeth. Then she said to Mary,
"God has blessed you more than
any other woman! He has also

blessed the child you will have.
Why should the mother of my
Lord come to me? As soon as I
heard your greeting, my baby
became happy and moved within
me. The Lord has blessed you
because you believed that he will
keep his promise."

Joseph's Dream
Matthew 1:18-24

Mary was engaged to Joseph from King David's family. Because Mary learned that she was going to have a baby by God's Holy Spirit, Joseph decided to call off the wedding. Joseph was a good man and did not want to embarrass Mary in front of everyone.

While Joseph was thinking about this, an angel from the Lord came to him in a dream. The angel said, "Joseph, the baby that Mary will have is from the Holy Spirit. Go ahead and marry her. Then after her baby is born, name him Jesus, because he will save his people from their sins."

So the Lord's promise came true, just as the prophet had said, "A virgin will have a baby boy, and he will be called Immanuel," which means "God is with us."

Jesus Is Born

Luke 2:1-7

About that time Emperor Augustus gave orders for the names of all the people to be listed in record books. Everyone had to go to their own hometown to be listed. So Joseph had to leave Nazareth in Galilee and go to Bethlehem in Judea. Long ago Bethlehem had been King David's hometown, and Joseph went there because he was from David's family.

Mary traveled with Joseph to Bethlehem. She was soon going to have a baby. While they were there, she gave birth to her first-born son. She dressed him in baby clothes. Then she laid him on a bed of hay because there was no room for them in the inn.

The Shepherds

Luke 2:8-20

That night in the fields near Bethlehem some shepherds were guarding their sheep. All at once an angel came down to them from the Lord, and the brightness of the Lord's glory flashed around them. The shepherds were frightened.

The angel said, "Don't be afraid! I have good news for you, which will make everyone happy. This very day in King David's hometown a Savior was born for you. He is Christ the Lord. You will know who he is, because you will find him dressed in baby clothes and lying on a bed of hay."

Suddenly many other angels came down from heaven and joined in praising God. They said, "Praise God in heaven! Peace on earth to everyone who pleases God."

After the angels had left and gone back to heaven, the shepherds said to each other, "Let's go to Bethlehem and see

what the Lord has told us about."
They hurried off and found Mary
and Joseph.

When the shepherds saw
Jesus, they told his parents
what the angel had said about
him. Everyone listened and was
surprised. Mary kept thinking
about all this and wondering
what it meant. As the shepherds
returned to their sheep, they
were praising God and saying
wonderful things about him.
Everything they had seen and
heard was just as the angel had
said.

King Herod Hears about Jesus

Matthew 2:1-6

When Jesus was born in the village of Bethlehem in Judea, Herod was king.

During this time some wise men from the east came to Jerusalem and said, "Where is the child born to be king of the Jews? We saw his star in the east and have come to worship him." When King Herod heard about this, he was worried. So was everyone else in Jerusalem. Herod brought together the chief priests and the teachers of the Law of Moses and asked them, "Where will the Messiah be born?"

They told him, "He will be born in Bethlehem, just as the prophet wrote, 'Bethlehem in the land of Judea, you are very important among the towns of Judea. From your town will come a leader, who will be like a shepherd for my people Israel.'"

The Three Wise Men
Matthew 2:7-12

Herod secretly called in the wise men and asked them when they had first seen the star. Then Herod told them, "Go to Bethlehem and search carefully for the child. As soon as you find him, let me know. I want to go and worship him too."

The wise men listened to what the king said and then left. The star they had seen in the east went on ahead of them until it stopped over the place where the child was. They were thrilled and excited to see the star.

When the men went into the house and saw the child with Mary, they knelt down and worshiped him. They took out their gifts of gold, frankincense, and myrrh and gave them to him. Later they were warned in a dream not to return to Herod. They went back home by another road.

Jesus of Nazareth
Matthew 2:13-23; Luke 2:40

After the wise men had gone, an angel from the Lord appeared to Joseph in a dream and said, "Get up! Hurry and take the child and his mother to Egypt! Stay there until I tell you to return. Herod is looking for the child and wants to kill him."

That night, Joseph got up and took his wife and the child to Egypt. There they stayed until Herod died. So the Lord's promise came true, just as the prophet had said, "I called my son out of Egypt."

When Herod found out that the wise men from the east had tricked him, he was very angry. He gave orders for his men to kill all the boys who were two years old and younger living in or near Bethlehem.

After King Herod died, an angel from the Lord appeared in a dream to Joseph while he was still in Egypt. The angel said, "Get up and take the child and his mother back to Israel. The people who wanted to kill him are now dead."

Joseph got up and left with them for Israel. Then in a dream he was told to go to Galilee. They went to live there in the town of Nazareth. So the Lord's promise came true, just as the prophet had said, "He will be called a Nazarene."

The child Jesus grew. He became strong and wise, and God blessed him.

Jesus in the Temple

Luke 2:41-52

Every year Jesus' parents went to Jerusalem for Passover. When Jesus was twelve years old, they all went there as usual for the celebration. After Passover Jesus' parents left, but they did not know that Jesus had stayed on in the city. They thought he was traveling with some other people. They could not find him with their relatives and friends. So they went back to Jerusalem and started looking for him there.

Three days later they found Jesus sitting in the temple, listening to the teachers and asking them questions. Everyone who heard him was surprised at how much he knew and at the answers he gave. His mother said, "Son, why have you done this to us? Your father and I have been very worried. We have been searching for you!"

Jesus answered, "Why did you have to look for me? Didn't you know that I would be in my Father's house?" But they did not understand what he meant.

Jesus went back to Nazareth with his parents and obeyed them. His mother kept on thinking about all that had happened. Jesus became wise and strong. God was pleased with him and so were the people.

John the Baptist
John 1:19-28

The Jewish leaders in Jerusalem sent priests and temple helpers to ask John who he was. He told them plainly, "I am not the Messiah." When they asked him if he were Elijah, he said, "No, I am not!" And when they asked if he were the Prophet, he also said "No!"

Finally they said, "Who are you then? We have to give an answer to the ones who sent us. Tell us who you are!" John answered in the words of the prophet Isaiah, "I am only someone shouting in the desert, `Get the road ready for the Lord!'"

Some Pharisees had also been sent to John. They asked him, "Why are you baptizing people, if you are not the Messiah or Elijah or the Prophet?"

John told them, "I use water to baptize people. But here with you is someone you don't know. Even though I came first, I am not good enough to untie his sandals." John said this as he was baptizing east of the Jordan River in Bethany.

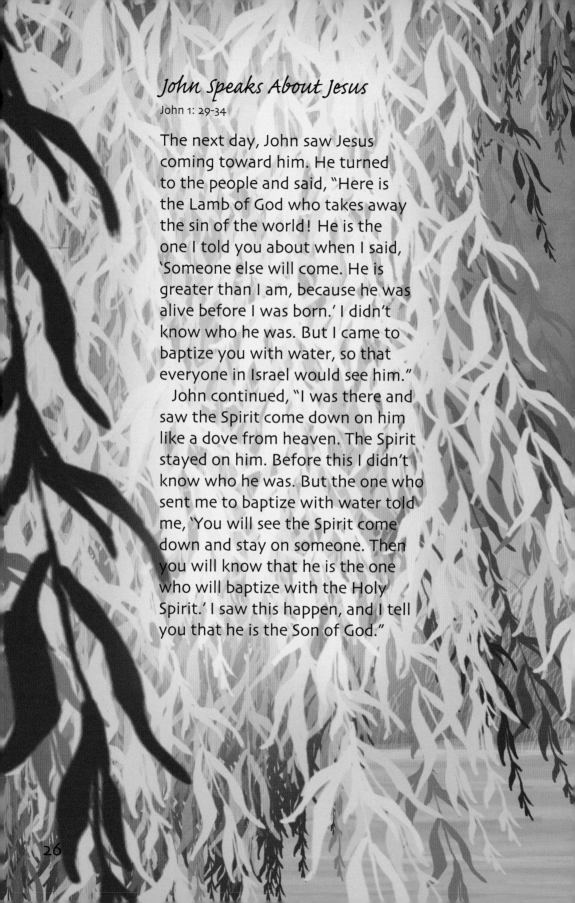

John Speaks About Jesus

John 1: 29-34

The next day, John saw Jesus coming toward him. He turned to the people and said, "Here is the Lamb of God who takes away the sin of the world! He is the one I told you about when I said, 'Someone else will come. He is greater than I am, because he was alive before I was born.' I didn't know who he was. But I came to baptize you with water, so that everyone in Israel would see him."

John continued, "I was there and saw the Spirit come down on him like a dove from heaven. The Spirit stayed on him. Before this I didn't know who he was. But the one who sent me to baptize with water told me, 'You will see the Spirit come down and stay on someone. Then you will know that he is the one who will baptize with the Holy Spirit.' I saw this happen, and I tell you that he is the Son of God."

Jesus Is Baptized

Matthew 3:1-17

Years later, John the Baptist
started preaching in the desert
of Judea. He said, "Turn back to
God! The kingdom of heaven
will soon be here." John wore
clothes made of camel's hair. He
had a leather strap around his
waist and ate grasshoppers and
wild honey.

From Jerusalem and all Judea
and from the Jordan River
Valley crowds of people went to

John. They told John how sorry they were for their sins, and he baptized them in the river.

Jesus left Galilee and went to the Jordan River to be baptized by John. But John kept objecting and said, "I ought to be baptized by you. Why have you come to me?"

Jesus answered, "For now this is how it should be, because we must do all that God wants us to do." John agreed. So Jesus was baptized.

As soon as Jesus came out of the water, the sky opened. He saw the Spirit of God coming down on him like a dove. Then a voice from heaven said, "This is my own dear Son, and I am pleased with him."

The Devil Tempts Jesus

Luke 4:1-15

When Jesus returned from the Jordan River, the power of the Holy Spirit was with him, and the Spirit led him into the desert. For forty days Jesus was tested by the devil. During that time he went without eating. When it was all over, he was hungry. The devil said to Jesus, "If you are God's Son, tell this stone to turn into bread."

Jesus answered, "The Scriptures say, 'No one can live only on food.'"

Then the devil led Jesus up to a high place and quickly showed him all the nations on earth. The devil said, "I will give all this power and glory to you. It has been given to me, and I can give it to anyone I want to. Just worship me, and you can have it all."

Jesus answered, "The Scriptures say, 'Worship the Lord your God and serve only him!'"

Finally, the devil took Jesus to Jerusalem and had him stand on top of the temple. The devil said, "If you are God's Son, jump off. The Scriptures say, 'God will tell his angels to take care of you. They will catch you in their arms, and you will not hurt your feet on the stones.'" Jesus answered, "The Scriptures also say, 'Don't try to test the Lord your God!'"

After the devil had finished testing Jesus in every way possible, he left him. Jesus returned to Galilee with the power of the Spirit. News about him spread everywhere. He taught in the Jewish meeting places, and everyone praised him.

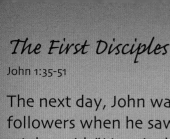

The First Disciples
John 1:35-51

The next day, John was with two of his followers when he saw Jesus walking by.

John said, "Here is the Lamb of God!" John's two followers heard him, and they went with Jesus. When Jesus turned and saw them, he asked, "What do you want?"

They answered, "Rabbi, where do you live?" The Hebrew word "Rabbi" means "Teacher."

Jesus replied, "Come and see!"

It was already about four o'clock in the afternoon when they went with him and saw where he lived. So they stayed on for the rest of the day. One of the two men who had gone with Jesus was Andrew, the brother of Simon Peter. The first thing Andrew did was to find his brother and tell him, "We have found the Messiah!" The Hebrew word "Messiah" means the same as the Greek word "Christ." Andrew brought his brother to Jesus. When Jesus saw him, he said, "Simon son of John, you will be called Cephas." This name can be translated as "Peter."

Jesus Chooses Philip and Nathanael

John 1: 43-51

Jesus decided to go to Galilee. There he met Philip, who was from Bethsaida, the hometown of Andrew and Peter. Jesus said to Philip, "Come with me." Philip found Nathanael and said, "We have found the one that Moses and the Prophets wrote about. He is Jesus, the son of Joseph from Nazareth."

Nathanael asked, "Can anything good come from Nazareth?"

Philip answered, "Come and see."

When Jesus saw Nathanael coming toward him, he said, "Here is a true descendant of our ancestor Israel. And he isn't deceitful."

"How do you know me?" Nathanael asked.

Jesus answered, "Before Philip called you, I saw you under the fig tree." Nathanael said, "Rabbi, you are the Son of God and the King of Israel!"

Jesus answered, "Did you believe me just because I said that I saw you under the fig tree? You will see something even greater. I tell you for certain that you will see heaven open and God's angels going up and coming down on the Son of Man."

Fishers of Men

Luke 5:1-11

Jesus was standing on the shore of Lake Gennesaret. He was teaching the people as they crowded around him to hear God's message. Near the shore he saw two boats left there by some fishermen who had gone to wash their nets. Jesus got into the boat that belonged to Simon and asked him to row it out a little way from the shore. Then Jesus sat down in the boat to teach the crowd.

When Jesus had finished speaking, he told Simon, "Row the boat out into the deep water and let your nets down to catch some fish."

"Master," Simon answered, "we have worked hard all night long and have not caught a thing. But if you tell me to, I will let

36

the nets down." They caught so many fish that their nets began ripping apart. Then they signaled for their partners in the other boat to come and help them. The men came, and together they filled the two boats so full that they both began to sink. When Simon Peter saw this happen, he knelt down in front of Jesus and said, "Lord, don't come near me! I am a sinner."

Peter and everyone with him were completely surprised at all the fish they had caught. His partners James and John were surprised too. Jesus told Simon, "Don't be afraid! From now on you will bring in people instead of fish." The men pulled their boats up on the shore. Then they left everything and went with Jesus.

37

Jesus Turns Water into Wine

John 2:1-11

Mary, the mother of Jesus, was at a wedding feast in the village of Cana in Galilee. Jesus and his disciples had also been invited and were there.

When the wine was all gone, Mary said to Jesus, "They don't have any more wine." Jesus replied, "Mother, my time hasn't yet come! You must not tell me what to do." Mary then said to the servants, "Do whatever Jesus tells you to do."

At the feast there were six stone water jars that were used by the people for washing themselves in the way that their religion said they must. Each jar held about twenty or thirty gallons. Jesus told the servants to fill them to the top with water. Then after the jars had been filled, he said, "Now take some water and give it to the man in charge of the feast." The servants did as Jesus told them.

The man in charge drank some of the water that had now turned into wine. He did not know where the wine had come from, but the servants did. He called the bridegroom over and said, "The best wine is always served first. Then after the guests have had plenty, the other wine is served. But you have kept the best until last!"

This was Jesus' first miracle. Jesus showed his glory, and his disciples put their faith in him.

Jesus Visits the Temple

John 2:13-22

Not long before the Jewish festival of Passover, Jesus went to Jerusalem. There he found people selling cattle, sheep, and doves in the temple. He also saw moneychangers sitting at their tables. Jesus took some rope and made a whip. He chased everyone out of the temple, together with their sheep and cattle. He turned over the tables of the moneychangers and scattered their coins. Jesus said to the people who had been selling doves, "Get those doves out of here! Don't make my Father's house a marketplace."

The Jewish leaders asked Jesus, "What miracle will you work to show us why you have done this?"

"Destroy this temple," Jesus answered, "and in three days I will build it again!" The leaders replied, "It took forty-six years to build this temple. What makes you think you can rebuild it in three days?"

But Jesus was talking about his body as a temple. When he was raised from death, his disciples remembered what he had told them. Then they believed the Scriptures and the words of Jesus.

41

Jesus and Nicodemus

John 3:1-6; 16-21

There was a man named Nicodemus who was a Pharisee and a Jewish leader. One night he went to Jesus and said, "Sir, we know that God has sent you to teach us. You could not work these miracles, unless God were with you." Jesus replied, "I tell you for certain that you must be born from above before you can see God's kingdom!"

Nicodemus asked, "How can a grown man ever be born a second time?"

Jesus answered, "Before you can get into God's kingdom, you must be born not only by water, but by the Spirit. Humans give life to their children. Yet only God's Spirit can change you into a child of God."

Then Jesus continued, "God loved the people of this world so much that he gave his only Son. Everyone who has faith in him will have eternal life and never really die. God did not send his Son into the world to condemn its people. He sent him to save them!

"The light has come into the world, and people who do evil things are judged guilty because they love the dark more than the light. People who do evil hate the light and won't come to the light, because it clearly shows what they have done. But everyone who lives by the truth will come to the light, because they want others to know that God is really the one doing what they do."

The Water of Life

John 4:4-26

This time Jesus had to go through Samaria. On his way he came to the town of Sychar. It was near the field that Jacob had long ago given to his son Joseph. The well that Jacob had dug was still there. Jesus sat down beside it because he was tired from traveling. It was noon and Jesus' disciples had gone into town to buy some food.

Just then, a Samaritan woman came to draw water from the well. Jesus asked her, "Would you please give me a drink of water?"

"You are a Jew," she replied, "and I am a Samaritan woman. How can you ask me for a drink of water when Jews and Samaritans won't have anything to do with each other?" Jesus answered, "You don't know what God wants to give you, and you don't know who is asking you for a drink. If you did, you would ask me for the water that gives life."

"Sir," the woman said, "you don't even have a bucket, and the well is deep. Where are you going to get this life-giving water?" Jesus answered, "Everyone who drinks this water will get thirsty again. But no one who drinks the water I give will ever be thirsty again. The water I give is like a flowing fountain that gives eternal life."

The woman said, "I know that the Messiah will come. He is the one we call Christ. When he comes, he will explain everything to us."

"I am that one," Jesus told her, "and I am speaking to you now."

45

The Samaritans Believe

John 4:27-42

The disciples returned and were surprised to find Jesus talking with a woman. But none of them asked him what he wanted or why he was talking with her. The woman left her water jar and ran back into town. She said to the people, "Come and see a man who told me everything I have ever done! Could he be the Messiah?" Everyone in town went out to see Jesus. While this was happening, Jesus' disciples were saying to him, "Teacher, please eat something." But Jesus told them, "I have food that you don't know anything about." His disciples started asking each other, "Has someone brought him something to eat?" Jesus said, "My food is to do what God wants! He is the one who sent me, and I must finish the work that he gave me to do."

A lot of Samaritans in that town put their faith in Jesus because the woman had said,

"This man told me everything I have ever done." They came and asked him to stay in their town. Jesus stayed on for two days. Many more Samaritans put their faith in Jesus because of what they heard him say. They

told the woman, "We no longer have faith in Jesus just because of what you told us. We have heard him ourselves, and we are certain that he is the Savior of the world!"

Jesus Heals an Official's Son

John 4: 43-54

Jesus had said, "Prophets are honored everywhere, except in their own country." Then two days later he left and went to Galilee. The people there welcomed him, because they had gone to the festival in Jerusalem and had seen everything he had done.

While Jesus was in Galilee, he returned to the village where he had turned the water into wine. There was an official whose son was sick. When the man heard that Jesus had come from Judea, he went and begged him to keep his son from dying.

Jesus told the official, "You won't have faith unless you see miracles and wonders!"

The man replied, "Lord, please come before my son dies!"

Jesus then said, "Your son will live. Go on home to him." The man believed Jesus and started back home. Some of the official's servants met him along the road and told him, "Your son is better! The fever left him yesterday at one o'clock."

The boy's father realized that at one o'clock the day before, Jesus had told him, "Your son will live!" So the man and everyone in his family put their faith in Jesus.

This was the second miracle that Jesus worked after he left Judea and went to Galilee.

The Power of the Son

John 5: 19-30

Jesus told the people, "I tell you for certain that the Son cannot do anything on his own. He can do only what he sees the Father doing, and he does exactly what he sees the Father do. The Father loves the Son and has shown him everything he does. The Father will show him even greater things, and you will be amazed. Just as the Father raises the dead and gives life, so the Son gives life to anyone he wants to.

"The Father doesn't judge anyone, but he has made his Son the judge of everyone. The Father wants all people to honor the Son as much as they honor him. Everyone who hears my message and has faith in the one who sent me has eternal life and will never be condemned. They have already gone from death to life.

"I tell you for certain that the time will come, and it is already here, when all of the dead will hear the voice of the Son of God. And those who listen to it will live! The Father has the power to give life, and he has given that same power to the Son. And he has given his Son the right to judge everyone, because he is the Son of Man. Everyone who has done good things will rise to life, but everyone who has done evil things will rise and be condemned. I cannot do anything on my own. The Father sent me, and he is the one who told me how to judge. I judge with fairness because I obey him. I don't just try to please myself."

Witnesses for Jesus

John 5: 31-47

Jesus continued, "If I speak for myself, there is no way to prove I am telling the truth. But there is someone else who speaks for me, and I know what he says is true. You sent messengers to John, and he told them the truth. John was a lamp that gave a lot of light, and you were glad to enjoy his light for a while.

"But something more important than John speaks for me. I mean the things that the Father has given me to do! All of these speak for me and prove that the Father sent me. The Father who sent me also speaks for me, but you have never heard his voice or seen him face to face. You have not believed his message, because you refused to have faith in the one he sent.

"I don't care about human praise. You like to have your friends praise you, and you don't care about praise that the only God can give! Don't think that I will be the one to accuse you to the Father. You have put your hope in Moses, yet he is the very one who will accuse you. Moses wrote about me, and if you had believed Moses, you would have believed me. But if you don't believe what Moses wrote, how can you believe what I say?"

Jesus Heals a Crippled Man

Luke 5:17-26

One day some Pharisees and experts in the Law of Moses sat listening to Jesus teach. They had come from every village in Galilee and Judea and from Jerusalem. Some people came carrying a crippled man on a mat. They tried to take him inside the house and put him in front of Jesus. But because of the crowd, they could not get him to Jesus.

The men carried the crippled man up on the roof. They removed some tiles and let the mat down in the middle of the room. When Jesus saw how much faith they had, he said to the crippled man, "My friend, your sins are forgiven." The Pharisees and the experts began arguing, "Jesus must think he is God! Only God can forgive sins."

Jesus knew what they were thinking, and he said, "Why are you thinking that? Is it easier for me to tell this crippled man that his sins are forgiven or to tell him to get up and walk? But now you will see that the Son of Man has the right to forgive sins here on earth."

Jesus then said to the man, "Get up! Pick up your mat and walk home."

At once the man stood up in front of everyone. He picked up his mat and went home, giving thanks to God. Everyone was amazed and praised God. What they saw surprised them, and they said, "We have seen a great miracle today!"

Jesus Will Return to the Father

John 7: 32-36

When the Pharisees heard the crowd arguing about Jesus, they got together with the chief priests and sent some temple police to arrest him. But Jesus told them, "I will be with you a little while longer, and then I will return to the one who sent me. You will look for me, but you won't find me. You cannot go where I am going."

The Jewish leaders asked each other, "Where can he go to keep us from finding him? Is he going to some foreign country where our people live? Is he going there to teach the Greeks? What did he mean by saying that we will look for him, but won't find him? Why can't we go where he is going?"

Nicodemus Stands up for Jesus

John 7:42-52

Some of the people in the crowd said, "The Scriptures say that the Messiah will come from the family of King David. Doesn't this mean that he will be born in David's hometown of Bethlehem?" The people started taking sides against each other because of Jesus. Some of them wanted to arrest him, but no one laid a hand on him.

When the temple police returned to the chief priests and Pharisees, they were asked, "Why didn't you bring Jesus here?" They answered, "No one has ever spoken like that man!" The Pharisees said to them, "Have you also been fooled? Not one of the chief priests or the Pharisees has faith in him. And

these people who don't know the Law are under God's curse anyway."

Nicodemus was there at the time. He was a member of the council, and was the same one who had earlier come to see Jesus. He said, "Our Law doesn't let us condemn people before we hear what they have to say. We cannot judge them before we know what they have done." Then they said, "Nicodemus, you must be from Galilee! Read the Scriptures, and you will find that no prophet is to come from Galilee."

59

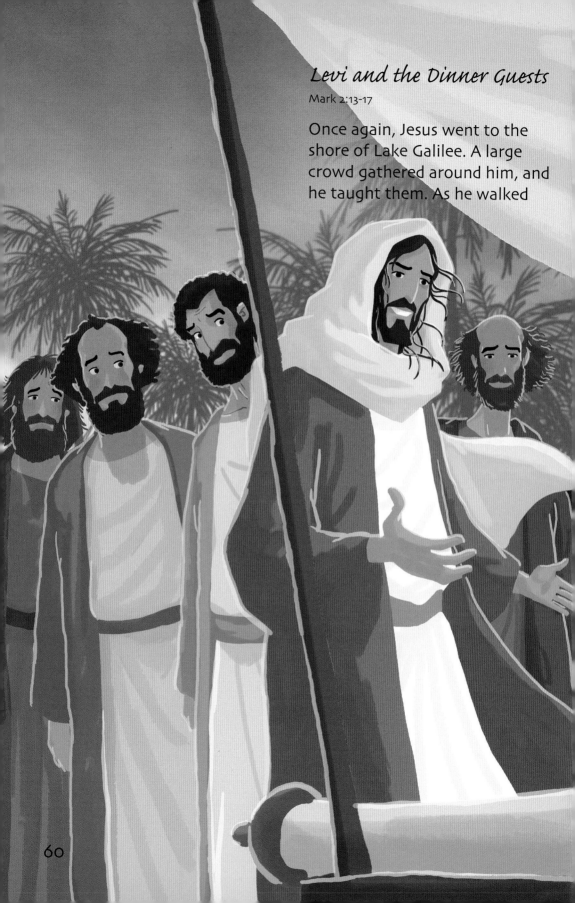

Levi and the Dinner Guests

Mark 2:13-17

Once again, Jesus went to the shore of Lake Galilee. A large crowd gathered around him, and he taught them. As he walked along, Jesus saw Levi, the son of Alphaeus. Levi was sitting at the place for paying taxes. Jesus said to him, "Come with me!" So Levi got up and went with Jesus.

Later, Jesus and his disciples were having dinner at Levi's house. Many tax collectors and other sinners had become followers of Jesus, and they were also guests at the dinner. Some of the teachers of the Law of Moses were Pharisees, and they saw that Jesus was eating with sinners and tax collectors. They asked his disciples, "Why does he eat with tax collectors and sinners?" Jesus heard them and answered, "Healthy people don't need a doctor, but sick people do. I didn't come to invite good people to be my followers. I came to invite sinners."

The Contemporary Bible Series